STANDING IN THE FOREST
OF BEING ALIVE

More Praise for Katie Farris'

STANDING IN THE FOREST
OF BEING ALIVE

"The real genius of *Standing in the Forest of Being Alive* is how Katie Farris' poems orbiting her cancer continuously turn toward wonder, deep wonder made wise by having known profound suffering: "One must train oneself to find, in the midst of hell, / what isn't hell." The poems braid the incessant urgent demands of a sick body with the incessant urgent demands of a sick country, a dying earth. The effect is brilliant, vertiginous—but also kind of shockingly readable and, importantly, often really funny. Farris has given us a truly wise, unforgettable, delight-full book."

—KAVEH AKBAR, author of the award-winning *Calling a Wolf a Wolf*

"Precise, imaginative, full of life: in the midst of shock and pain, this book rings with love of language."

—RAE ARMANTROUT, author of Pulitzer-Prize winning *Versed*

"*One must train oneself to find, in the midst of hell, what isn't hell*, Farris writes in her poem... finding one's way through the inferno of cancer survival, of writing despite and with the body, commending to paper the luminous terror of having come through."

—CAROLYN FORCHÉ, Pulitzer-Prize finalist for *In the Lateness of the World*

"With its immersive magic and unforgettable imagery, life surges through this gorgeous book that rewards and rewards."

—*THE LITERARY REVIEW*

"Farris writes a gorgeous self-elegy: 'I will need a rope/to let me down into the earth./I've hidden others/strategically around the globe,/a net to catch/my body in its weaving.' She provides an account of the dailiness of illness, long after the visitors disappear. With signature wit, Farris engages in a power struggle with mortality and in the end, her ferocity and conviction win through language that sings."

—VICTORIA CHANG, author of the nationally acclaimed *Obit*

STANDING
IN THE
FOREST
OF
BEING ALIVE

A MEMOIR IN POEMS

Katie Farris

Alice James Books
NEW GLOUCESTER, MAINE
alicejamesbooks.org

CELEBRATING 50 YEARS OF ALICE JAMES BOOKS

10 9 8 7 6 5 4 3 2 1

Alice James Books are published by Alice James Poetry Cooperative, Inc.

Alice James Books
Auburn Hall
60 Pineland Drive, Suite 206
New Gloucester, ME 04260
www.alicejamesbooks.org

Library of Congress Cataloging-in-Publication Data

Names: Farris, Katie, author.
Title: Standing in the forest of being alive : a memoir in poems / Katie Farris.
Description: New Gloucester, Maine : Alice James Books, [2023]
Identifiers: LCCN 2022040943 (print) | LCCN 2022040944 (ebook) | ISBN
9781948579322 (trade paperback) | ISBN 9781949944235 (epub)
Subjects: LCSH: Farris, Katie--Poetry. | Breast--Cancer--Treatment--Poetry.
| LCGFT: Autobiographical poetry.
Classification: LCC PS3606.A746 S73 2023 (print) | LCC PS3606.A746
(ebook) | DDC 811/.6--dc23/eng/20220922
LC record available at https://lccn.loc.gov/2022040943
LC ebook record available at https://lccn.loc.gov/2022040944

Alice James Books gratefully acknowledges support from individual donors, private
foundations, the National Endowment for the Arts, and the Amazon Literary
Partnership. Funded in part by a grant from the Maine Arts Commission, an
independent state agency supported by the National Endowment for the Arts.

Cover photograph by Anne Sullivan

Table of Contents

Why Write Love Poetry in a Burning World

To train myself to find in the midst of hell
what isn't hell.

The body bald
cancerous but still
beautiful enough to
imagine living the body
washing the body
replacing a loose front
porch step the body chewing
what it takes to keep a body
going—

This scene has a tune
a language I can read a door
I cannot close I stand
within its wedge
a shield.

Why write love poetry in a burning world?
To train myself in the midst of a burning world
to offer poems of love to a burning world.

Tell It Slant

You float in the MRI gloam,
several spiculated masses;
I name you "cactus,"
carcinoma be damned—you make
a desert of all
of me.

Have I said it slant enough?
Here's a shot between
the eyes: Six days before
my thirty-seventh birthday,
a stranger called and said,
You have cancer. Unfortunately.
And then hung up the phone.

When You Walk over the Earth

When you walk over
the earth, it asserts
itself: *Here. Here.*

Here. It says to your
feet. You must reckon
with the earth, though it enters

you less (unless...). The sky always
has its hand in you,
as if you were a puppet,

through your ears down
your throat into your
lungs—and with the tips

of its fingers there, it caresses
every capillary, each blood cell,
until they blush.

On the Morning of the Port Surgery

Before dawn, I walk outside
the clock. I strip and fold
my clothes into a bag, surrender
my braid. I'm wheeled into
the operating theater
for the opening act of what
will become a defining role:
Cancer Patient, Stage 3.

O feather-headed mongrel
my pickled flea-bit heart
thrice sword-stabbed
please keep beating.

Ungraceful, the heart boinks:
  drugged, suspended, spiderwebbed—

In the Event of My Death

What used to be
a rope descending
my vertebrae to the basement
of my spine
grows thin.

In solidarity with my first chemotherapy
our cat leaves her whiskers on
the hardwood floor.
I gather them, each purewhite parenthesis,
and plant them
in the throat of the earth.

In quarantine
I learned to trim your barbarian
hair. Now it stands always on end:
a salute to my superior barbary skills. In the event
of my death, promise you will find my heavy braid
and bury it—

I will need a rope
to let me down into the earth.
I've hidden others
strategically around the globe,
a net to catch
my body in its weaving.

The Man You Are the Boy You Are

The man you are opens the door
to your anguish, a mirror

of my own—we've both grown
silver around the eyes. But in your pocket,

the boy you are brings me a melted
candy bar. You issue commands

like an old man, then take out
my trash like a young boy

with a crush.

If Marriage

If marriage
is a series
of increasing
intimacies, a slow
sweet collapse into
oneness, I
would still beg
your forgiveness
for asking
your assistance
unwinding that pale hair
from my hemorrhoid.

A Row of Rows

We argue on the front
porch: whose turn is it to lecture
the other? Fruit salad or
steak? And was Whitman
or Dickinson the greater
epic poet?

We argue (Whitman)
about the ripeness of
bananas, the rawness
of the meat, and whether
it's okay to throw apple
cores in the street (I hold
it's not).

A pleasant row
of rows, little tugs
on the strings
of our love,
just enough
to pull our days
taut.

In the Early Days of a Global Pandemic

In the early days of a global pandemic
I can't stop writing about love, while everyone

is writing about a country.
Everywhere in America (is everywhere

America, yet?)—in America,
which is to say, everywhere—

Americans are spreading rumors,
writing about a country as if a country existed

in the midst of a global pandemic, about its citizens
as if we were visible, while America, which is an idea

in our grasp, twists itself into an eagle,
condenses into a bowl of hot chicken soup,

then a factory never retrofitted to make ventilators, then a trillion
dollars, then fresh water, then saltwater,

then salt.

Finishing Emily Dickinson, First Deacon in William
Blake's Church of the Marriage of Heaven and Hell,
in the Oncologist's Waiting Room

Oh, Emily, goodbye!
We met in February and parted
in July—

I meet
your sweet velocity in every
thing that flies—

in mote
and star and sphere—in bird
and phosphorus of God!

Oblique, you preached obliquity—
your body, steeple for the Church of Mystery—
your bell rings on, beyond.

Outside Atlanta Cancer Care

I return to this point of wonder:

what kind of animal began to stand
on such small feet? And only two?
What vertical absurdity!
What upright madness!

Perhaps we were imitating the trees—
lifting our arms,
wishing for roots—
and then forgot to set ourselves
back down on our four, more
                              rational feet—

our longing grew our fingers longer,
twigs into branches—
for if you long hard enough,
do you not find fruit
in your palms?

I return to this point of wonder.

Eros Haiku

Today, my apple
core sat on the countertop
waiting for your mouth.

An Unexpected Turn of Events Midway through Chemotherapy

I'd like some sex please.
I'm not too picky—
    (after all, have you seen me?
    so skinny you could
    shiv me with me?)
Philosexical, soft and
Gentle, a real
Straight fucking, rhymed
Or metrical—whatever
You've got, I'll take it.
Just so long as we're naked.

Rachel's Chair

Once, many
years ago, we made
love at a friend's
house. We were over-
night guests, not
perverts (on the whole),
but what I am
trying to say is she
owned a chair so
perfect for lovemaking
we joked about asking
to take it home. If
I had only known, then,
how rarely we would find
such objects,

I would have.

The Invention of America

I am trying to be a love poet though I cannot escape
America it's as if I am married to
America and no one stood to object
America would have objected itself if
America wasn't so busy trying to jam
America on my finger later washing my hands
America rings as it lands on the porcelain
America and clatters down the silver throat of the
America I don't have a pipe wrench so
America arrives and saves the day leaving
America relieved to have
America returned to its
America where it reminds
America of
America.

*

Everyone is writing about a country
as if a country existed.

*

As an anti-capitalist act, I reject your hierarchies of worth, America—

All things are erotic.

O cockroach,
smooth as a lozenge, glossy

as hard candy, antennae
clever as spun
sugar, come
into my mouth.

*

I vote but prefer smut
        to politicians. You, "gentle" men!

*

Everyone is writing about America's citizens
as if they were visible:

Why write love poetry
in a time of
government brutality?

Can the clot prove
the heart's loyalty?
            Blocked,
beating the   harder:
love re-   doubling?

*

Everyone is writing about a country
as if a country existed.

Quid Pro Quo: A Dedication

You said
we could replace
our lumpy
twenty-year-old
mattress if
I wrote you
a poem.
So here's
your god-
damn
poem.

Pirate Haiku

4 am. His left
eye closes for the night; his
stubborn right? Reading.

Emiloma: A Riddle & an Answer

Will you be
my death, breast?
I had asked you
in jest and in response
you hardened—a test
of my resolve? Malignant
magnificent palimpsest.

                *

Will you be
my death, Emily?
Today I placed
your collected poems
over my breast, my heart
knocking fast
on your front cover.

                *

Will you be
my death, chemo?
The shell of my self
in the sphere of time
plucking, plucking
the wool of my hair
from its branches.

                *

Will you be
my death, Emily?
And keep the sky
from reaching inside—
you, the voice; me, the faithful echo?
Will you be
my death, echo?

*

Do you know—*no*
in which meadow—*mow*
the gingko grows—*goes*
which is fallow, which furrowed—*foes*
what is winnowed, what is—*woe.*

Ode to Money, or Patient Appealing Health Insurance for Denial of Coverage

I don't know what money is. Moss? The mink's crescent
teeth? Or maybe money is
the morning I woke
at dawn to wander
past the orange
blossoms, a smell with four
      dimensions, touching me through
time. Is that

        currency?

My uncle, Christopher Marlowe,
mad, drank the visions until he died.
                You bury
treasure.

To determine a family's net
value, make a list of assets, then subtract
liabilities. Asset: Geraldine Fox's 1948 degree in
chemistry. Liability: William Marlowe's propensity
for hurting his daughter. Am I doing this right? Is this

        the gold standard?

Asset: seeing light that isn't there,
like a ship passing through the narrow harbors
of my eyes, scraping—
                is burying treasure a cash

transaction?

I once buried a half-
decayed skunk I fished from my Uncle Christopher's
garbage can, covered in bees. X marks the spot.

In sum: perhaps the moon's an insurance adjustor.

America's optimistic to dye its money
green. Leaves are green
because of chlorophyll, which is the machine
that turns sunlight, water, and carbon dioxide into leaf, stem, and root. All
the little blades of grass left behind by the lawn mower like Civil
War soldiers.   Same as cash.

             A heavy-bodied moth
caught between glass and screen casts its shadow   down
into the palm of my hand: one dark coin.

A Week before Surgery, I Practice My Body

like Giotto's angels, sketched from his studies
of sheep, I open the jaws of my back to the sky,

eating my body deeper into this blue—
like Jonah vomited from the whale, fragrant

as ambergris. Or plain as any woman who,
a week before mastectomy, practices being opened.

I Wake to Find You Wandering the Museum of My Body

Twenty-four Greek urns
Painted with wrestling boys
Comprise my spine.

Unusually well-preserved, my
Feet are the elaborate slippers
Of a beloved Chinese concubine,

Heavily embroidered
With vein and shadow.
My bald head? A lofty sunlit dome
Lined with pietà after

Pietà, every mourning
Virgin great in grief and
Execution.

My organs are
The furniture galleries
Everyone skips, but for you,
Carpenter, standing

Guilt-fingered before
My heart's armoire,
Stroking always toward the grain.

Come to Me

Come to me,
Sleeplit,
Warm as a
Burrow—
Salt lick
And sweet
As a boy.

Come to me,
Griefsplit,
Backward
As bones.
Yourself an
Avalanche
From the cliffs

Of yourself—

To the Pathologist Reading My Breast, Palimpsest

(written with Kimberly Point du Jour, MD)

Specimen B, received fresh and subsequently placed in formalin,
consists of a 392 g, 18 x 15.5 x 3 cm simple oriented mastectomy.

Dear Doctor—you've done my work for me in your first line
with your tidy slanting rhyme of *specimen* and *formalin.*

To rhyme *mastectomy,* I thought my dear friend's pregnancy;
she and I, our birthdays, two slender months apart—

both of us harboring rapidly dividing cells, so near our hearts.
How's that for art?

Present on the anterior surface is a tan grossly unremarkable
skin ellipse with an eccentric, soft everted nipple.

Beneath my *grossly unremarkable skin ellipse*
an inscription there of every kiss

a couple (playful) too-hard twists
and late-night drunken dare-you strips.

But mostly, my own homely grip
as I skidded into sleep.

Five Days before the Mastectomy, Insurrection at the Capitol

What is the door
the bullet makes
in the body?

America, the gun—
predictable, mechanical,
possessed of several chambers—
if I reside right by your side,
must I expect your dangers?

Who holds you holstered
America the gun?

What is the door the bullet
makes in the body? What do we
call it? Body?

After the Mastectomy

At the oncologist's office, a man stares. I stare back
until he says, "People must stare at you."

Why bother closing a door
when everyone demands it open?

I go to the world with my tongue out
and my shirt unbuttoned, my keys

in the lock,
a six-inch scar instead of a nipple—

how can a watchtower hide?
I am well-positioned to seek out

fires and invading hoards—
my bald head the beacon the first

alarm.

Woman with Amputated Breast Awaits PET Scan Results

The waiting, sleek as otters, slips
between your lips.

Without the waiting, who can know when spring will come, or snow?
Heading south, the geese all beat
the waiting with their wings.

Turn on the light at 2 am;
the waiting stands, hand
on your head. A most maternal haunting.

Swimming, the human body humps along: each dive in time
ends so close to its beginning.

Help me to spell waiting? I forget. And whom
can I tell how much I want to live? I want to live.

A stone, the waiting weights my body into stone:
what's left, almost a palindrome.

Woman with Amputated Breast at her Mother-in-Law's Grave

1.

A grave is
a door
we open.

In my dream,
his mother Ella curls
into my body,
bald as a breast.

2.

What if the past
is a crouching tiger
and memory is the act
of putting your head
in its mouth?

3.

Thank you
for the turkey I forgot
to take out of the freezer; for your forgiveness
and for the lamb in the deli drawer.
Thank you for what eats,
and for the dead, and for
what eats the dead—

all of us,
whether fertile whether fallow,
fodder.

4.
This elastic earth:
with little ceremony,
how it expands.

5.
A grave is
a door
we open,
lay our dead down in,
begging
like a key begs
           a keyhole—

Thank you, grief—
whose root is love— and love
which has teeth, and
eats.

Ilya, Orphaned, after the Bough Fell through Our Roof

Looking up through the hole in our roof,
you never expected this inheritance:

never expected this blue, here, or for your house
to be frame for the sky—yet birds sleep under the

sky each night; their bones
as fine as the clappers of tiny bells.

The Wheel

One must train oneself to find, in the midst of hell,
what isn't hell.

For instance, the way you folded love into a booklet
and gave it to me to read.

What isn't hell is your big belly now—
how it rounds itself: my hemisphere.

Ugly gardenias and muggy
sunsets, horizon glowing orange as a riot: all these I find,

and they are not hell.
I like a pebble in my mouth,

how it tastes like beets.
I like beets, how they taste like dirt

and cool white wine,
drinking as your fingers work their way

between stockings and thigh.
To train myself to find

in the midst of hell what isn't hell, I grub at the roots
of words (your dirty Latin)—finding a mouse

in Russia's armpit, or the doll baby
in the deep black pupil of an Englishman's

eye. What is not hell is whispering, *I like my body
when it's with your body*; the way

the poet Cummings, a manikin,
crawls from between my teeth and

over my lip, watching us, his hands down
the front of his pants.

I like the wheel   I like its flame how
it crushes and uplifts in one motion

how its hub is the pupil of everyone's eye

                                        how we're all afraid

to die how we go down   howling

beating the   drums of our   own
bodies—

Woman with Amputated Breast Returns for her Injection

Now I lack the muscle to pull me into the third dimension,
but in these two I can give you the world!
Three drains, five scans, twenty thousand dollars!
Come, Doctor, how do you like me now—

I never wanted to be anything but biddable.
You see the outline of my shape? Fill it in with
your pencils, seven points tickling me with color.

I can! I can! I can can-can!
Watch me can! Watch me do! Watch me has!
Watch me watch!
This cancer patient has ambition—

I scratch and scratch and here we are, dancing the chart—
when you give me that Zoladex shot,
it's from one long needle, and right in the gut.

Standing in the Forest of Being Alive

I stand in the forest of being alive:
in one hand, a cheap aluminum pot
of chicken stock and in the other,
a heavy book of titles. O once, walking through
a cemetery, I became terribly lost and could not
speak (no one living knows the grammar).
No one could direct me to the grave,
so I looked at every name.

A heavy bird flapped its wings over someone's
sepulcher. Some of us are still putzes
in death, catching bird shit on our headstones.
Some of us never find what we're looking for, praying
it doesn't pour before we find our names; certain
we're headed in the right direction, a drizzle begins,
and what's nameless inside our veins
fluoresces, fluoresces in the rain.

Irony

Gout lacquers
his foot scarlet:
a stoplight, a gaudy
lump. He holds
it up like a prize,
cannot bear
hiding it under
sock or sheet.

The irony, of course,
is sweet: the poor
refugee, who hates
beer, and meat—
the peasant boy
who, in his feet,
carries the rich
man's disease.

He hands it to me
like a cup of crystal.
Take it! he says,
so I hold it to my ear:
my telephone.

Scheduling the Bone Scan

The word "bone" tolls in your ear,
a bell. What tolls? The word, the bone?

The drum in your ear moves the hammer
like a lever, a bone moves
the word "bone" through your ear.

You repeat "bone," your voice droning—
not silver: bronze. A duller thud.
Nothing ringing—instead, a buzz—
the devouring sound—the insect, time.

Contrition

At the twenty-
fifth twitch of
the blanket, his thirty-
ninth minute
testicular adjustment,

I snapped and whacked
his shoulder. Contrite now,
I push my face against his face,

say, *Dream of water, my love.*
And we both let go
our moorings.

In the Shadow of This Valley

I'd like to write you something mighty,
a quake to send all your books of love poems flying
like paper birds around your head,
and the photographs of your exes
pecking at our words, flocking
to the windows—voyeurs.

(Why do love poems attract birds
as sure as seed or worm or nectar?)

Soon, my love poem will settle,
but for an aftershock or two; soon it will
become solid ground, and we'll be
puzzled, looking down, to remember
the love poem from long ago,
how it shook.

Said the High Priestess to the Magician

I'm designed
for alone;
a lighthouse, I say,
his arm around
me, arabesque.
    (His word; too
    fluty for me.)

He shifts, adds
the flourish of his other
arm to my sans
serif self, smiles
through my grump.
He *joys* me, reluctant, pulls
laughter,

that
redvioletorangecerulean
handkerchief,
slowly,
right
out of my
mouth.

Against Loss

I don't remember this December on the precipice
of holiday: your hair poorly cut, the pile of calico fur between
my right shoulder and your left, purring.
                    The year and the truck out back
both idling,   idling and dying.

                    This memory I do not have—
I would like to give it to you,
            a prophylactic against loss:

just   four arms and four
paws and eight legs. Just six lungs,
sending our breath to the air,
                              just
the air.

To the God of Radiation

Given the unexpected choice between
uncertain death and certain damage,
I find in the mirror a woman—breastless, burned— who,
in an advisory capacity,
asks, *How much do you*
want to live?

Enough.

O God of Radiation,
let your light
like a ship pass through me,
your radiance exposing,
exposing what's inside me
like film a god takes—

but must you clatter the eaves
of my scapula, scurry
the grasshopper nest of my heart, scythe my nerves
and cobweb my muscles
to the rungs
of my ribs? How much more can one body take?

Enough.

Light every deadly cell like a wick
burning in the paper lantern of my chest—

my chest, a thing
so ephemeral
yet held so firmly in your fist.

Ice for Me

Some say the world will end in fire...
—Robert Frost

but if it's not cancer, it will be ice
for me, Robert. A long
cold sleep on the hairy chest
of the forest, tugged and tickled
by beasts to death, yes:
I'll walk willingly between
the curtains of the trees.

What Would Root

Walking through a cathedral of oak trees
and bristlecone pines, scolded by squirrels
in their priestly black, their white collars
wagging with the force of their scolding, I
was struck simultaneously, in both eyes,
by some sort of flying detritus—pollen or seeds—
and stopped to lean against a rock
to scrub it (I thought) away. It was May,

it was May, it was May, and the air was sweet
with pine and island mountain lilac. The squirrels
(I mentioned them already, etc.), and the lizards
ran down the spines of rocks like a bad feeling. I
could see everything: redheaded hummingbirds
dipped their beaks into the little red hoods of penstemon
and I, a redhead, could hear everything: a red-crested
woodpecker who was not offended I did not know his name.

Everything smelled green: it was all green, really—
even the red was anti-green, and though my eyes
ached from everything-seeing, I could taste the granite
in the spring (oh yes I drank water from the ground; I
was wild even then, though the squirrels scolded
me and tried to convince me I was not). Soon I crested
a rise; the land spread itself greenly for me and I
wished I had seed to toss into that green, just to see

what would root. My right eye would not close to this
view (why would it?) but when I reached up to touch it I

felt a twig emerging, and another from my
other eye; that they were a part of my body I could not doubt—
they were living and enervated and jutting out. I
sat down feeling the hairs on the back of my neck
understanding for the first time they were not hairs, but roots.
Everything was everything: the twigs in my eyes

tasted sunlight with my mouth, the roots drew the salt
from my sweat into their vacuum, and I was no longer hungry.
Everything; it was all green; the roots in my skull shifted and I
lay down beneath my own branches. I had to wiggle a bit to
find a place to lay my head: the rock was very hard
and I needed softer ground—yes, a place for the top
of my head to come off, to nuzzle into the earth, to drink.

Acknowledgments

For my mother, who also had young breast cancer, who teaches me to advocate for myself, assuages those fears that can be assuaged, and helps me bear the burden of those fears that remain.

For Eli, who blazed a trail for armpit cancer in the face of doctors and nurses who didn't understand; for his kindness and gentleness and badass activism; for being a soul sibling.

For everyone whose life has been touched by this complex and devastating disease, and especially for the researchers trying to unwind the mystery.

For the mystery.

"In the Event of My Death" first appeared in *The Nation*, thanks to Kaveh Akbar.

"What Would Root" first appeared in *Poetry*, thanks to Don Share.

"Standing in the Forest of Being Alive," "To the Pathologist Reading My Breast, Palimpsest," "Woman with Amputated Breast Returns for her Injection," & "Ice for Me" first appeared in *American Poetry Review*, thanks to Elizabeth Scanlon.

"Rachel's Chair" was featured in *Poetry Daily*, thanks to Peter Streckfus.

"Why Write Love Poetry in a Burning World," "On the Morning of the Port Surgery," "The Man You Are the Boy You Are," & "If Marriage" first appeared in *Granta* (UK), thanks to Rachael Allen.

"I Wake to Find You Wandering the Museum of My Body" first appeared in *Massachusetts Review* as "An Untitled Collection of Generalizations That Mobilize the Eye," thanks to Ellen Doré Watson.

"When You Walk over the Earth" first appeared in *Ecotone*, thanks to Anna Lena Phillips Bell.

"If Marriage" & "Rachel's Chair" first appeared in *Prairie Schooner*, thanks to Kwame Dawes.

"Emiloma: A Riddle & an Answer" first appeared in *Rumpus*, thanks to Carolina Ebeid.

"Said the High Priestess to the Magician" first appeared in *Yes Poetry*, as "The Magician Meets the High Priestess," thanks to Joanna C. Valente and Stephanie Valente.

Many of the poems in this book appeared in the chapbook *A Net to Catch My Body in Its Weaving*, winner of the Chad Walsh Chapbook Prize and published by *Beloit Poetry Journal*.

"Why Write Love Poetry in a Burning World" and "Standing in the Forest of Being Alive" were both recipients of the 2023 Pushcart Prize.

Many of these poems were written at the Virginia Center for Creative Arts.

Thanks to Kaveh Akbar, fairy godmother of this book.

Thanks to Jessica Jacobs, who wrestled many of the poems in this book into shape like the angel wrestled Jacob.

Thanks to Carey Salerno, who believed; Julia Bouwsma, who refined; and Alyssa Neptune, who had infinite patience; and for everyone at Alice James Books and Pavilion Poetry/Liverpool University Press. I am continually humbled by and grateful for your work and passion.

To my doctors: Erin Bowman, Otto Metzger, David Raque, Mylin Torres, and Amelia Zelnak, and to consulting physician João Luís Barreto Guimarães.

To my radiation techs, especially Jody Miles, my nurses, especially Laura Walsh, and to my physical therapist Bernice Cohen.

Immense gratitude to: Sandra Alcosser, Rae Armantrout, Anna Lena Phillips Bell, Brody Bernheisel, Olga Bragina, Joanna Brooks, Jericho Brown, Nickole Brown, Elena Karina Byrne, James Byrne, Victoria Chang, Mario Chard, Eileen Chong, Pura López Colomé, Gary Dop, Halina Duraj, Brian Evenson, Carrie Erving, Nihad Farooq, Carolyn Forché, Katie Ford, Carol Frost, Richard Frost, Jeannine Hall Gailey, Rachel Galvin, Forrest Gander, Danielle Hanson, Karen Head, Brian Henry, Edward Hirsch, Jane Hirschfield, Ishion Hutchinson, Sabine Huynh, Alex Irigoyen, Jessica Jacobs, David Keplinger, Lauren Klein, Aviya Kushner, Jeffrey Levine, Paige Lewis, Olga Livshin, Sabrina Orah Mark, Maya Marshall, Maureen McLane, Todd Michney, Jenny Minniti-Shippey, Malena Mörling, Valzhyna Mort, Mihaela Moscaliuc, Jocelyn Ou, Sandeep Parmar, Eli Patterson, Deryn Rees-Jones, JC Reilly, Tatiana Retivov, Susan Rich, Leslie Shipman, Suzanne Simmons, Maggie Smith, Jim Sparrell, Tedward Speck, Peter Streckfus, Anne Sullivan, Katie Towler, Adam Veal, Randi Ward, Laurie Watel, Michael Waters, Ellen Doré Watson, Eleanor Wilner, Christian Wiman, Cecilia Woloch, Greg Zinman, and so many others who helped shape this book, and who helped to support me as I was undergoing treatment for breast cancer.

Recent Titles from Alice James Books

Alice James Books is committed to publishing books that matter. The press was founded in 1973 in Boston, Massachusetts to give women access to publishing. As a cooperative, authors performed the day-to-day undertakings of the press. The press continues to expand and grow from its formative roots, guided by its founding values of access, excellence, inclusivity, and collaboration in publishing. Its mission is to publish books that matter and preserve a place of belonging for poets who inspire us. AJB seeks to broaden our collective interpretation of what constitutes the American poetic voice and is dedicated to helping its artists achieve purposeful engagement with broad audiences and communities nationwide. The press was named for Alice James, sister to William and Henry, whose extraordinary gift for writing went unrecognized during her lifetime.

Designed by Tiani Kennedy

Printed by McNaughton & Gunn